A Quick Reference Guide to
Angels in the Bible

Also by Kermie Wohlenhaus, Ph.D.

How to Talk and Actually Listen to Your Guardian Angel
The Complete Reference to Angels in the Bible

A Quick Reference Guide to
Angels in the Bible

Kermie Wohlenhaus, Ph.D.

Kermie & the Angels Press   Tucson, Arizona

Copyright © 2014 by Kermie Wohlenhaus, Ph.D.

All rights reserved. No part of this book may be reproduced or transmitted in any form or by any means, electronic or mechanical, including photocopying, recording, or by any information storage and retrieval system, without permission in writing from the author.

Scriptures are taken from the King James Version of the Bible. All other versions of the Bible, except the New King James Version, tend to alter the references to angels and use other names for these heavenly hosts. This has caused reference guides to miss important verses regarding the angels.

To contact the author or order
additional copies of this book
Kermie & The Angels Press
P. O. Box 64282
Tucson, AZ 85728
www.KermieandtheAngels.com
KermieandtheAngels@gmail.com

This edition was prepared for publication by
Ghost River Images
5350 East Fourth Street
Tucson, Arizona 85711
www.ghostriverimages.com

Cover design by Kermie Wohlenhaus

ISBN: 978-0-9832300-2-1
Library of Congress Control Number: 2014908235

Printed in the United States of America
First Printing: May, 2014
10 9 8 7 6 5 4 3 2 1

Dedicated to the Divine and the Glorious Angels

Table of Contents

Introduction	9
Angels of the Angelic Hierarchy	13
Seraphim	13
Cherubim	13
Thrones	15
Dominions	15
Powers	15
Principalities	16
Archangels	17
Michael	17
Gabriel	18
Angels in the Old Testament	19
Angels in the Psalms	21
Angels in the New Testament	23
Angels in the Life of Jesus in Chronological Order	23
Jesus's Teachings Regarding the Angels	25
Acts of the Apostles, Paul's Letters, the General Letters	26
Angels in The Book of Revelation	29
About the Author	31

Introduction

There are over 180 scriptures regarding angels in the Bible. Many biblical scholars and theologians have glossed over the importance of these celestial beings in biblical dissertation and study. But now the study of angels – Angelology – is bringing these winged emissaries of the Divine back into focus and illuminating their great work in our sacred texts.

The word angel – from the Greek word "angelos" – is derived from the Hebrew "malakh" meaning "messenger." Angels are not limited to being *only* "messengers" of Divine Will, but are also known to be helpers, rescuers and guides – clearing the way. Angels were created by the Divine to fulfill Divine Will between God and creation. They talk to us in dreams and manifest physically. They come to give great proclamations and are known to punish, liberate and often save us.

We read in the New Testament that angels were very involved in the life of Jesus. They not only came to his unwed mother and proclaimed his conception, but were present at Jesus's birth, ministered to him throughout his life and were on hand to explain Christ's resurrection at the tomb.

A Quick Reference Guide to Angels in The Bible is an easy, fast way to find verses regarding angels in the Bible. To have the full scriptures in their complete form, please refer to *The Complete Reference to Angels in The Bible* by Kermie Wohlenhaus, Ph.D. Both are the perfect complement to any biblical study of angels.

This book begins with "Angels of the Angelic Hierarchy" created by Pseudo-Dionysius from Syria in the 6th Century. The Roman Catholic Church, which was the authorizing Christian Church for many decades, has used this Angel Hierarchy of angel orders and choirs since that time. Other Christian angelologists continue to utilize this as an important, but not the only, theory to this day. Because of its popularity, I have opened this reference guide with "Angels of the Angelic Hierarchy". They are: Seraphim, Cherubim, Thrones, Dominions, Powers, Principalities, Archangels (including Michael and Gabriel) and, of course, the Angels.

The next section is "Angels in the Old Testament" including "Angels in the Psalms". This is followed by "Angels in the New Testament," highlighting "Angels in the Life of Jesus In Chronological Order", "Jesus's Teachings Regarding the Angels" and the "Acts of the Apostles, Paul's Letters and the General Letters." This quick reference guide finishes with "Angels in the Book of Revelation."

We read that angels not only protect but liberate, minister, prophesize, praise God and walk with us unawares. They also punish, kill and stop us and the donkey we are riding on in our tracks if they have a Divine reason for doing so. They are mighty and filled with Divine power and love.

I hope this booklet will encourage study and illuminate the Divine work that these great beings of light perform in our lives.

May the angels continue to shower you with Divine blessings,

Kermie Wohlenhaus, Ph.D.
www.KermieandtheAngels.com

Angels of the Angelic Hierarchy

Seraphim

Isaiah 6:1-13 - Description of Seraphim and Holy Song

Revelation 4:1-11 - Four Living Creatures (Seraphim) Give Glory to God and Holy Song

Cherubim

Genesis 3:1-24 - Cherubim Guarding with a Flaming Sword the Tree of Life and the Garden of Eden

Exodus 25:16-22 - Two Cherubim of Gold in the Two Ends of the Mercy Seat and Upon the Ark of the Testimony
Exodus 26:1-37 - Make the Tabernacle with Cherubim of Cunning Work and With Cherubim Shall it Be Made
Exodus 36:1-38 - Tabernacle Made with Cherubims of Cunning Work
Exodus 37:1-29 - He Made Two Cherubims of Gold, Beaten Out of One Piece at Two Ends of the Mercy Seat

Cherubim (cont.)

Numbers 7:89 - One Speaking to Moses from off the Mercy Seat from between Two Cherubims

1 Samuel 4:1-22 - Ark of the Covenant which Dwells between Cherubims

2 Samuel 6:1-23 - Ark of God that Dwells between the Cherubims

1 Kings 6:11-38 - Two Cherubims Carved Out of Olive Wood
1 Kings 7:13-36 - On the Borders that were between Ledges were Cherubims and on Plates of the Border's Ledges
1 Kings 8:1-24 - The Most Holy Place, Even Under the Wings of Cherubims and Spread Forth their Two Wings

2 Kings 19:1-37 - Lord God of Israel which Dwells between Cherubims

1 Chronicles 13:1-14 - Ark of God that Dwells between Cherubims
1 Chronicles 28:1-21 - Chariot of the Cherubims that Covered the Ark of the Covenant of the Lord

2 Chronicles 3:1-17 - Graved Cherubims on the Walls and Most Holy House, Two Cherubims Description
2 Chronicles 5:1-14 - Cherubims Spread their Wings over the Ark

Psalms 80 - Shepherd of Israel, Thou that Dwells between Cherubims
Psalms 99 - Lord Reigns and Sits between the Cherubims

Isaiah 37:1-38 - Lord of Hosts, God of Israel that Dwells between Cherubims

Ezekiel 10:1-22 - Position, Appearance and Duties of the Cherubims

Ezekiel 11:14-25 - The Cherubims Lift up their Wings

Ezekiel 41:1-26 - Cherubims and Palm Trees with Every Cherub had Two Faces

Hebrews 9:1-28 - Cherubims of Glory Shadowing the Mercy Seat

Thrones

Ezekiel 1:1-28 - Description of Thrones in a Vision of Enoch

Daniel 7:1-28 - Daniel Beheld till the Thrones were Cast Down

Colossians 1:9-18 - All Things Created, Thrones, Dominions or Principalities

Dominions

Daniel 7:1-28 - The Kingdom and Dominion

Colossians 1:9-18 - All Things Created, Thrones, Dominions or Principalities

Powers

Matthew 24:1-37 - Immediately after the Tribulation . . . the Powers of Heavens shall be Shaken

Mark 13:1-37 - The Stars of Heaven shall Fall and the Powers that are in Heaven shall be Shaken

Powers (cont.)

Romans 8:35-39 - For I am Persuaded, that neither Death . . . nor Powers

Romans 13:1-8 - Let Every Soul be Subject unto the Higher Powers

Ephesians 3:1-12 - To the Intent that now unto the Principalities and Powers in Heavenly Places might be Known

Ephesians 6:10-13 - For we Wrestle not against Flesh and Blood but against Powers

Colossians 1:9-17 - For by Him were All Things Created, that are in Heaven . . . whether they be . . . or Powers

Colossians 2:8-17 - And Having Spoiled Principalities and Powers

Titus 3:1-7 - To be Subject to Principalities and Powers

Hebrews 6:1-6 - Have Tasted the Good Word of God and the Powers of the World

1 Peter 3:18-22 - Powers being Made Subject unto Him

Principalities

Jeremiah 13:16-18 - Your Principalities shall Come Down, even the Crown of Your Glory

Romans 8:35-39 - For I am Persuaded that neither Death nor Principalities

Ephesians 3:1-12 - Now unto the Principalities and Powers in Heavenly Places be Known by the Church, the Manifold Wisdom

Ephesians 6:10-13 – For we Wrestle not against Flesh and Blood but against Principalities

Colossians 1:9-17 - All Things Created whether they be Principalities

Colossians 2:8-17 - Having Spoiled Principalities

Titus 3:1-7 - To be Subject to Principalities and Powers

Archangels

1 Thessalonians 4:13-18 - The Lord shall Descend from Heaven with the Voice of the Archangel

Revelation 8:1-2 - I Saw Seven Angels which Stood before God (Commonly thought to be the Seven Archangels in Christian Theology)

Michael

Daniel 10:1-21 - Michael shall Stand Up and none that Hold with Me these Things but Michael your Prince

Daniel 12:1-3 - Michael Stand Up, the Great Prince

Jude 1:1-9 - Michael the Archangel Disputed about the Body of Moses

Revelation 12:1-10 - Michael and his Angels Fought against the Dragon

Gabriel

Daniel 8:1-27 - Gabriel, Make this Man to Understand the Vision
Daniel 9:20-27 - Gabriel being Caused to Fly Swiftly and Touched Me

Luke 1:1-38 - Gabriel Speaking to Zachariah about Birth of Son John and Gabriel Proclaiming the Birth of Jesus to Mary

Angels in the Old Testament

Genesis 16:1-16 - Angel of the Lord Aiding Hagar and Ishmael
Genesis 19:1-28 - Two Angels to Sodom and Gomorrah
Genesis 21:1-21 - Angel of God Rescues Hagar and Ishmael
Genesis 22:1-18 - Angel of the Lord Stops Abraham from Slaying Isaac
Genesis 24:1-67 - Angel Finds Isaac's Wife
Genesis 28:1-22 - Angels of God Descending and Ascending on Jacob's Ladder
Genesis 31:1-13 - Jacob Explaining Dream from the Angel of God
Genesis 32:1-3 - Jacob Met Angels of God
Genesis 48:1-22 - Israel (Jacob) Asking Angel Blessing for Joseph

Exodus 3:1-22 - Moses and Angel of the Lord in Burning Bush
Exodus 14:1-31 - Angel of God Went before the Camp of Israel
Exodus 23:19-33 - God Sending an Angel before Moses and Israel
Exodus 32:1-35 - God Sending an Angel before Moses and Israel
Exodus 33:1-3 - God Sending an Angel to Drive Out the Inhabitants of the Promised Land

Numbers 20:1-17 - Moses' Messengers Retelling Story of God Sending an Angel Leading Israel out of Egypt
Numbers 22:1-41 - Balaam and the Angel of the Lord

Angels in the Old Testament (cont.)

Judges 2:1-7 - Angel of the Lord Prophesying about Israel's Disobedience to Joshua and Israelites
Judges 5:1-31 - Deborah's Song including a Verse about the Angel of the Lord
Judges 6:1-40 - Gideon and the Angel of the Lord
Judges 13:1-25 - Angel of the Lord Prophesying Samson's Birth

1 Samuel 29:1-11 - Achish Calling David as an Angel of God

2 Samuel 14:1-23 - Joab Sending Wise Woman to King David - Wise as the Wisdom of an Angel of God
2 Samuel 19:24-27 - Mephibosheth Saying the King is Like the Angel of God
2 Samuel 24:1-25 - Angel of the Lord Destroying Jerusalem

1 Kings 13:1-34 - Bethel Lying about what Angel told Him
1 Kings 19:1-21 - Angel of the Lord helps Elijah to Escape

2 Kings 1:1-18 - Angel of the Lord gives Elijah a Message
2 Kings 19:1-37 - Angel of the Lord Kills 185,000 Assyrians

1 Chronicles 21:1-30 - King David and the Census of Israel - as Punishment, Angel of the Lord Destroys Jerusalem

2 Chronicles 32:1-33 - Isaiah Prays for Help and the Lord sent an Angel

Job 4:1-21 - Eliphaz tells Job, God Charges Angels with Folly

Ecclesiastes 5:1-7 - What Not to Say before the Angel

Isaiah 37:1-38 - Angel of the Lord Kills 185,000 Assyrians
Isaiah 63:1-19 - Angel of His Presence Saved the Afflicted

Daniel 3:1-30 - Nebuchadnezzar Praises God and Angel for Delivering Shadrach, Meshach and Abed-Nego from Fiery Furnace
Daniel 6:1-28 - Angel Shut the Lions' Mouths for Daniel

Hosea 12:1-14 - Hosea Saying that Jacob Struggled with the Angel

Zechariah 1:1-21 - Zechariah's Visions of Angels
Zechariah 2:1-13 - Zechariah's Visions of Angels
Zechariah 3:1-10 - Zechariah's Visions of Angels
Zechariah 4:1-14 - Zechariah's Visions of Angels
Zechariah 5:1-11 - Zechariah's Visions of Angels
Zechariah 6:1-15 - Zechariah's Visions of Angels
Zechariah 12:1-14 - Zechariah's Visions of Angels

Angels in the Psalms

Psalm 8 - Humans a Little Lower than Angels
Psalm 34 - Angel of the Lord Encamps and Delivers Those Who Revere God
Psalm 35 - Let the Angel of the Lord Chase and Persecute Those Who Fight Against Me
Psalm 68 - Thousands of Angels
Psalm 78 - Manna, the Bread of Angels
Psalm 91 - God Gives Angels Charge Over You to Keep You in All Your Ways
Psalm 103 - Bless the Lord, Ye Angels

Angels in the Psalms (cont.)

Psalm 104 - Who Makes God's Angels Spirits; Ministers of Flaming Fire
Psalm 148 - Praise God, All God's Angels

Angels in the New Testament

Angels in the Life of Jesus in Chronological Order

Luke 1:1-45 - Angel of the Lord Proclaims Birth of Son to Zacharias and Gabriel Foretells to Mary the Gender, Name, Destiny and that the Conception of her Child, Jesus, was from the Holy Ghost

Matthew 1:17-25 - Angel of the Lord in a Dream told Joseph about Taking Mary as His Wife and that the Baby was Conceived by the Holy Ghost and told Him the Child's Gender, Name and Destiny

Luke 2:1-20 - Angel of the Lord Announces the Birth of Jesus to the Shepherds, followed by a Multitude of Angels Praising God

Matthew 2:1-23 - Joseph Instructed in a Dream by the Angel of the Lord to Flee to Egypt and when to Return Safely to Israel

Mark 1:9-13 - Angels Ministered to Jesus after the 40-day Temptation

Matthew 4:1-11 - Angels Ministered to Jesus after the 40-day Temptation

Angels in the Life of Jesus in Chronological Order (cont.)

John 5:1-9 - Angel Troubled the Water at the Healing Pool in Bethesda

Luke 22:39-47 - Jesus Comforted by an Angel in His Agony at Mount of Olives

Matthew 28:1-8 - Angel of the Lord Rolled Back the Stone from Jesus' Tomb and Announced Jesus' Resurrection to the Women at the Tomb

John 20:1-18 - Angels Question Mary Magdalene's Grief at the Tomb

Matthew 13:1-58 – Parable of the Seeds and Angels to Harvest Righteous and Unrighteous for Jesus at the End of the Age

Matthew 24:25-31 - Jesus will Send His Angels with a Great Sound of a Trumpet to Gather His Elect

Mark 13:21-27 - He Shall Send His Angels to Gather Together His Elect

Mark 8:34-38 - Jesus Comes with the Holy Angels

Matthew 16:24-28 - The Son of Man Shall Come in the Glory of His Father with His Angels

Matthew 25:31-46 - Son of Man Shall Come in His Glory and all the Holy Angels; He shall Separate Them One from Another

Luke 9:18-26 - He Shall Come in His Own Glory and of the Holy Angels

Revelation 5:1-14 - Many Angels Praise the Lamb

Revelation 12:1-17 - Michael and His Angels Cast Out Dragon

Jesus's Teachings Regarding the Angels

Matthew 18:1-10 - In Heaven, Children's Angels Do Always Behold the Face of God

Matthew 22:23-30 - Angels of God Do Not Marry

Matthew 24:34-37 - Angels of Heaven Do Not Know all that God Knows – Time of Jesus' Coming

Matthew 26:46-56 - Jesus Could Pray to God and God Would Send 12 Legions of Angels (72,000) to Save Him

Mark 12:18-25 - Angels Do Not Marry

Mark 13:31-33 - Angels Do Not Know all that God Knows – Time of Jesus' Coming

Luke 9:23-27 - Whosoever Shall be Ashamed of Me . . . of Him Shall the Son of Man be Ashamed When He Comes in His Own Glory and of the Holy Angels

Jesus's Teachings Regarding the Angels (cont.)

Luke 12:8-12 - Whosoever Confesses Me before Men, Him Shall the Son of Man Also Confess before the Angels of God

Luke 15:1-10 - There is Joy in the Presence of Angels of God over One Sinner that Repents

Luke 16:14-31 - The Humble Beggar Lazarus Carried by the Angels into Abraham's Bosom

Luke 20:27-36 - Angels Do Not Marry Nor Do They Die

John 1:44-51 - Ye Shall See Heaven Open and the Angels of God Ascending and Descending upon the Son of Man

Acts of the Apostles, Paul's Letters, the General Letters

Acts 5:12-29 - Angel of the Lord Frees the Apostles from Prison
Acts 6:1-15 - Saw Stephen's Face as it Had Been the Face of an Angel
Acts 7:22-40 - Stephen's Defense Against Charges Recounting the Angel of the Lord in the Burning Bush Appearing to Moses and Spoke to Him on the Mount of Sinai
Acts 7:46-53 - Stephen Refers to Law Given by the Disposition of Angels
Acts 8:25-39 - Angel of the Lord Instructs Philip to Meet Ethiopian Eunuch
Acts 10:1-35 - Angel of God Came to Cornelius the Centurion to Send for Peter

Acts 11:1-18 - Peter Repeats to the Apostles and Brethren his Story about Cornelius and Gentiles Granted Repentance unto Life

Acts 12:1-25 - Peter being Rescued from Prison by the Angel of the Lord

Acts 23:1-11 - Paul being Questioned by Pharisees and Sadducees; Sadducees say that there are No Angels and Pharisees Defend Paul and say there are Angels

Acts 27:1-44 - Paul Being Told by Angel of God that Ship would be Lost, but No Loss of Life

Romans 8:35-39 - Paul Asking who shall Separate them from the Love of Christ? Not Angels

1 Corinthians 4:4-10 - Paul Saying how Apostles are made Spectacles unto the World and to the Angels

1 Corinthians 6:1-8 - Paul Warns to not Judge and Telling Apostles that They shall not Judge Angels

1 Corinthians 11:1-16 - Paul Instructs Women Covering their Heads while Praying and Prophesying because of the Angels

1 Corinthians 13:1-3 - Speaking with the Tongues of Angels

2 Corinthians 11:1-15 - Satan being Transformed into an Angel of Light

Galatians 1:1-8 - Paul Instructing the Church that We or an Angel Preach any Other Gospel, let Him be Accursed

Galatians 3:18-20 - Paul Speaking of the Law Being Ordained by Angels in the Hand of a Mediator

Galatians 4:6-14 Paul is Received as an Angel of God

Acts of the Apostles, Paul's Letters, the General Letters (cont.)

Colossians 2:16-19 - Paul Warning to Let no Man Begile You of Your Reward in the Worshipping of Angels

2 Thessalonians 1:3-10 - When Jesus Shall be Revealed from Heaven with His Mighty Angels
1 Timothy 5:17-25 - Paul Charging Timothy to Carry out his Instructions by Jesus Christ and the Elect Angels

Hebrews 1:1-14 - Jesus Made Better than Angels, Let All the Angels of God Worship Him and Sit on Right Hand of God and Ministering Spirits of the Heirs of Salvation
Hebrews 2:1-18 - Word Spoken by Angels and Made Him a Little Lower than the Angels
Hebrews 12:18-24 - Innumerable Company of Angels in Heaven
Hebrews 13:1-2 - Entertain Strangers, Unwittingly Entertain Angels

1 Peter 1:1-12 - Angels Desire to Look into those Things Preached
1 Peter 3:18-22 - Angels Subject to Jesus Christ

2 Peter 2:1-10 - God not Sparing Punishment on the Angels who Sinned

Jude 1:1-6 - Angels who did not Keep their Proper Domain

Angels in The Book of Revelation

Revelation 1:1-20 - Jesus Christ Sent and Signified Angel with this Revelation – Seven Stars = Seven Angels of the Seven Churches and Seven Candlesticks = Seven Churches

Revelation 2:1-29 - The Angel of the Church of Ephesus, Smyrna, Pergamo and Thyatira Writes

Revelations 3:1-22 - The Angel of the Chruch of Sardis, Philadelphia and Laodicean Writes

Revelation 5:1-14 - Strong Angel Proclaiming Who is Worthy to Open the Book - Many Angels Around the Throne Praising God and the Lamb

Revelation 7:1-17 - Four Angels Standing on the Four Corners of the Earth, Another Angel Ascending from the East, Crying not to Hurt the 144,000 - All Angels Around the Throne Worshipping God

Revelation 8:1-13 - Seven Angels Which Stood Before God and Sound Four of Seven Trumpets

Revelation 9:1-21 - Three More Angels Which Stood Before God and Sound Trumpets

Revelation 10:1-11 - A Mighty Angel Came Down From Heaven

Revelation 11:1-19 - Seventh Angel Sounded

Revelation 12:1-17 - Heavenly War between Michael and His Angels Fought Against the Dragon

Angels in The Book of Revelation (cont.)

Revelation 14:1-20 - Angels in the Midst of Heaven
Revelation 15:1-8 - Seven Angels and the Seven Plagues
Revelation 16:1-21 - Seven Angels and the Seven Plagues
Revelation 17:1-18 - Seven Angels and the Seven Vials
Revelation 18:1-24 - Angel Come Down From Heaven
Revelation 19:1-21 - Angel Calling Standing in the Sun
Revelation 20:1-15 - Angel Casting Down Satan for 1,000 Years
Revelation 21:1-27 - Seven Angels and the Seven Vials
Revelation 22:1-21 - John Worshipping at the Feet of the Angel

About the Author

Kermie Wohlenhaus, Ph.D. is an author, TV producer and angelologist. She teaches workshops and classes, gives angel presentations nationally and hosts a TV show in Tucson, Arizona on public access called *Kermie & the Angels* which is available on YouTube. As an angelologist, Dr. Wohlenhaus is regularly being interviewed on TV, radio, podcasts, and for newspapers and magazines throughout the United States. She is popular in live performance and with radio and TV audiences for her accurate angel messages and knowledge. Dr. Wohlenhaus is the Founder and Director of the School of Angel Studies.

Dr. Wohlenhaus's first book *How to Talk and Actually Listen to Your Guardian Angel* is based on her popular workshop of the same name. This book is also available in Spanish, French, and German. Her second book, *The Complete Reference to Angels in the Bible* is the expanded, companion book to *A Quick Reference Guide to Angels in the Bible*. The forthcoming *Angels in Sacred Texts* includes not only Angels in the Bible, but many other angelic sacred texts.

Dr. Wohlenhaus received a Bachelor of Science (BS) from Colorado State University, a Master of Divinity (MDIV) from the Iliff School of Theology and a Doctor of Philosophy (Ph.D.) in Religion/Metaphysics at the College of Metaphysical Studies. She is currently living in Tucson, Arizona.

For further information: www.KermieandtheAngels.com

www.ingramcontent.com/pod-product-compliance
Lightning Source LLC
Chambersburg PA
CBHW060622070426
42449CB00042B/2476